In My Thoughts

Inspirational quotes

to awaken the mind

Virginia Martin

DEDICATION

To my unborn grandchild

Always and forever in my heart

Cherish every minute

Do not take anything or anyone

For granted

Cristina Chang-Bryant

In honor of my dear high school friend, Cristina, who died from cancer, I share the above quote she wrote. I have never known a sweeter soul. - VM

ACKNOWLEDGMENT

Thank you God for inspiring and
gifting me with the written word.

INTRODUCTION

Words, expressed in quotes,

have the power to unleash the mind

in all different directions.

Enjoy the quotes within, and

draw inspiration to write your own,

on the "Write Your Own Quote" pages

included in the book.

At the start of each day

Let God be first

Before the world

Time is like the wind

You do not see it

But it is always moving

Achieve what you believe

So believe big

Take risks

Take chances

Never look back

On what could have been

It is in the quality of moments

Not quantity

That memories

Are made

No expectations

No worries

Make laughter

Part of your

Day to day routine

The key to inner joy

Is to live each day

As an adventure

Cherish the moment and

Let the moment cherish you

Your kiss is enough to tell me

Everything I want to know

I am soothed by the rhythm of your

Breathing, and loved by

The beat of your heart

Expressing a dream in words

Makes it real

It comes alive

Becoming something to look forward to

You will only be defeated

If you stop dreaming

Pursue what you want with action

Not just words

The poet casts a magical spell

On the heart of the reader

That is not easily broken

Snippets of life

Happen in the blink of an eye

Let time not be wasted

Make each moment count

Love bursts

Like a rapid succession of fireworks

Not easily extinguished

Trying to ride out the storm alone

Leaves hope on neutral and

Faith playing hide and go seek

When intuition tells you

Not to give up

Stay the course

No matter how rough

Dive into God's word daily

It is the only way you can stay afloat

The entrepreneurial spirit awakens

At the dawn of each day

Pursuing the dream

That once got away

Inside yourself is the power to sparkle

Excavating the soul

Reveals the priceless gems

Under pressure inside you

Shut out the noise

And wait on the Lord to speak

Give more than you take

Extend your hand

And see what develops

Finish the race

No matter how bumpy the road

Fully embrace your life

And declare your place in it

Remember you are a work in progress

Don't let shame get in the way

Of your God given purpose

Any age is a good age

To live the life you want

When you stay in place

Your feet go to sleep

So get out of your comfort zone

And wake up

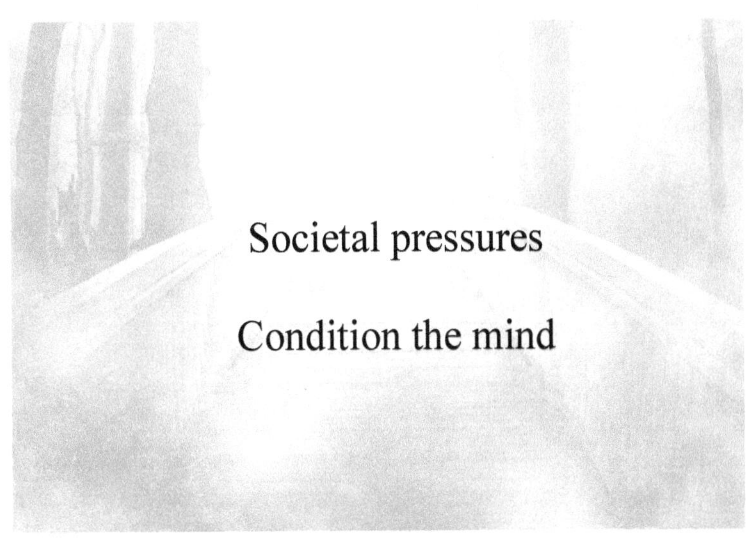

Societal pressures

Condition the mind

Kindness to strangers

Is a lasting legacy

Dreams become goals to go after

No more playing

By the rules of the game

Doing your work with pride

No matter what it is

Makes all the difference

I stand on my own

Not caring about winning a popularity

Contest or being a puppet

I am my own master

In the moment of trial

Whoever takes your hand

Is the one to trust

And hold close

The beating of my heart is in rhythm

With the drumming of your fingers

On my skin

Silence holds on long enough

For hearts to speak

You hold all the cards in your hand

Doing nothing

Is not how to play the game

The warmth of your breath

Tickles my neck

And I am no longer afraid

Love is unleashed

Even after life scars

Have tried to squash it

In life lessons

There is revelation

Bewilderment

Acceptance

There is no call to action

When something

Is only in the mind

Once it is in the heart

Then movement happens

Sincere and simple

Charismatic and sophisticated

Opposites complement

And love blooms

Trying to break someone who

Has been glued back together by God

Is like trying to fill a pitcher with water

That is full of cracks

Who am I?

But a servant of God

Willing to do

What He asks

Do not let fear control your aloneness

Know that you can step through it

At any moment

Even in the storm

I know

Love will find me

When I think I can stand on my own

Is when I fall

Keep the focus on God, not yourself

Only in God's arms

Can you really

Start to be healed

I will not make excuses for dreaming

Life goes on

Whether you are ready

For it or not

So pack a suitcase

Hold on to the rope of God's grace

Tears belong to yesterday

Faith is for today

Strength comes when I pray

Writing frees the mind

While music frees the soul

Love is a four letter word

That dissolves

In the mouth

Once it is said

Words help me speak my mind

When my lips are silent

A man who understands

Is like finding a diamond in the sand

The only way to heal

From something

Is to let it hurt

When we align ourselves with God

We see what He sees in us

We don't have

But a breath of time

To live this life

Let your mind fool your heart

From time to time

Awaken from a life of faking

Seal your fate with action

My soul creates with words

There is no other way

When one door shuts

Get on your knees and pray

Slowly, you feel

The breeze from an open window

When you feel like a trapped animal

Look for an escape

I write words that want

To have wings to fly

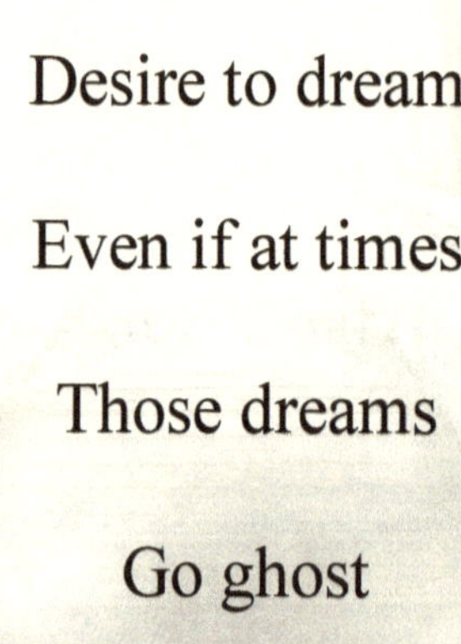
Desire to dream

Even if at times

Those dreams

Go ghost

We are each other's mess

So don't be afraid to get hurt

The heart only knows

That it beats with a kiss

Why *fall* in love?

When you can sing, dance, jump, walk

Or smile in love?

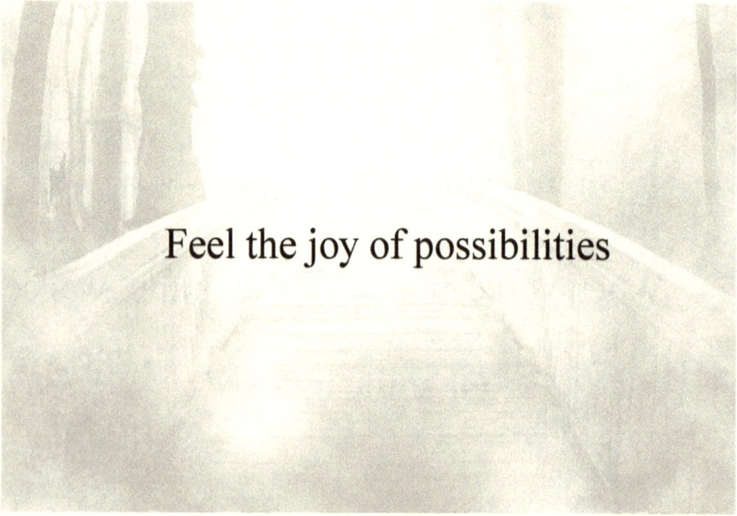

Feel the joy of possibilities

I need to escape in order to create

When God gives you the message to

"Be Still"

Brace for impact and

Keep the focus on Him

Good things

Are but

A flash in the journey

As short as life may be

Don't be a spectator

Jump from the sidelines

And get in the game

Details flow everywhere

Changing the course of your destination

Yet moving you forward anyway

Sometimes, it is in the losing someone

That you realize what you

Had won

Romance is the plan

Know how to allure what you want

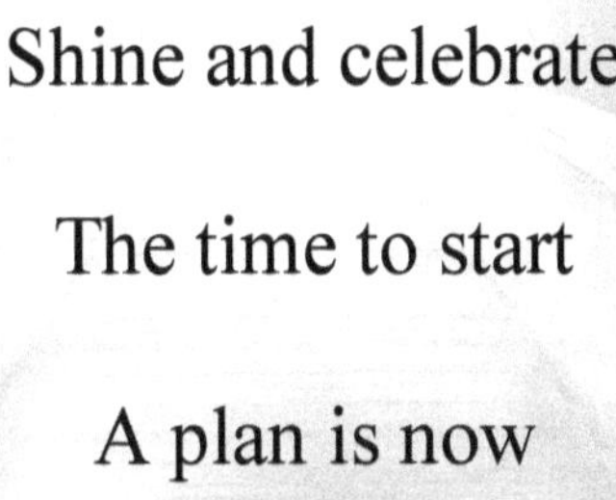
Shine and celebrate

The time to start

A plan is now

A moment of magic

Is to watch love grow

Memories are a unique

And endless mystery

I do not know how much

Under your spell I am

Just that the sound

Of your voice calms me

Inspiration leads you to imagine

An epic adventure

Extraordinary beginnings

Lead to beautiful endings

Take time to play

Look closer for a chance

To make fun experiences

Stay where life is inspiring

The bigger picture matters

Get ready to step

On greener grass more

Love is a song waiting to be sung

Love is playful and sweet

Do not mistake it for weakness

A creative mind is not organized

But, from chaotic thoughts

Writes a masterpiece

Love can be painted in many colors

My eyes tell no lies

They do not hide behind a smile

Do not shy away from someone's pain

Just take their hand

In quiet reassurance

That you love them

Stop and take the time

To heal that which causes you pain

You lose part of yourself

When you let go of love

You can get the best part of me

With an old-fashioned love song

Love's answer is to listen

And be immovable

The full power of love

Is to embrace the heart first

Cracks and all

The lovers' simple touch of hands

Is enough to know

They want to follow

The same path

The love left behind

Still breathes

As it waits for the one

That made it come to life

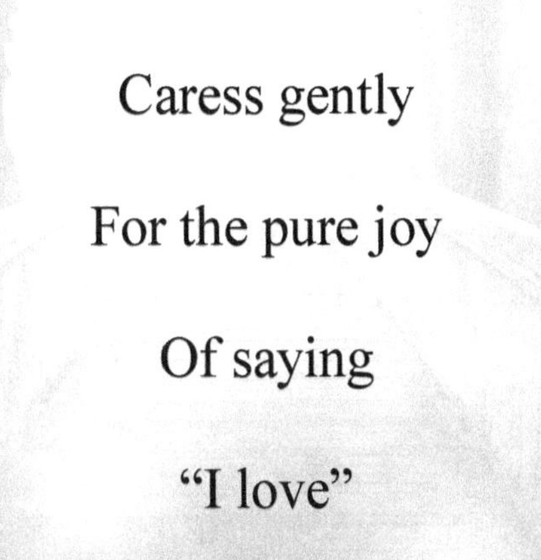
Caress gently

For the pure joy

Of saying

"I love"

Love takes root in nurturing soil

Whoever knows my song

Can help pull my heart back out

So it knows it is safe to love again

It is in the little things

That you can win someone's heart

Sometimes I want to color

The world with rainbows

So it can be a brighter place

Like a thief in the night

You come and steal my thoughts

I cannot tell you the day or the hour

When I think of you

I carry you in me always

Keep track of good family and friends

Share your journey with them

And let them in your story

Do not let looking back

Keep you from what is

In front of you

Write for the love of it

It is what you do with what you write

That determines what happens next

Words reach individuals

To encourage reading

(W.R.I.T.E.R.)

Let your creative mind

Have a fun day playing

With your imagination

Embrace the people in your life

Thank them for showing up

And being there

Get out of your comfort zone

So many beautiful things await

On the other side

Live your life to follow your dreams

What you hold in your heart manifests

Itself on the outside

That is why you look at someone within

Not out

When you are down on your luck

All you have to do is look up

God is listening

When you have a passion for something

Don't let anything get in the way

Of pursuing it

Aspire for greatness

Show up in the best way

You can possibly be

Writing takes things out of my head

Not my heart

For that I sing

Do not let the busyness of life

Get in the way

Of God sent opportunities

Inside you are the best pieces

Waiting to be unleased

My mind runs free

Minute by minute

Thoughts push in

Wanting to be heard

In the dark moments of your life

Trust God

To light the fire within

Love is as sweet as apple pie

With ice cream

We are here on Earth

For much more

Than we give ourselves credit for

Life is a continuous game

Set in motion

By that which

Makes you come alive

Faith is not a buzz word

It is a lifelong commitment

To the One true God

When love exists in the heart

It does not have to be found

When you realize there is

More to someone that meets the eye

It is time to let your guard down

And embrace their uniqueness

It is all about the dash in your life

And how well you live it

That makes all the difference

Dance to your favorite music

Sing a love song

Recite the words of a poem

Enjoy a well-acted play

Let the arts have their way with you

The emotion of a song

Has to touch the heart

In order to have meaning

Find someone that brings

Rhythm into your heart

I read to escape my mind

An awareness of anything

Is better than nothing

For it allows you to do something

I am drawn to the broken pieces of

Another's heart

Silence is the worst communicator

Love is a great motivator

Hope, love, inspire

No matter what is happening around you

Sometimes two people

Find each other

Through the chaos

And heal each other's hearts

Let hope always shine a light

Back to God

Clear your mind daily

To receive God's message

Impart knowledge and words of wisdom

That leave a timeless legacy

Rise up to what God has planned

So get out of your way to

Go out of your way for

God to lead the way

Give love a chance to be

Part of your life

Just have your eyes, as well as

Your heart open wide

Let your relationship with God

Never be compromised

By word, action, or deed

Train your body

Feed your spirit

I love you with an open hand

Not a tight fist

You can conquer the world

When your heart is singing

I am here on purpose

And nothing can take

That away from me

There are words that long to be written

And others that beg to be forgotten

Recharge yourself spiritually

Every morning

By reading God's word

When something does not move forward

It is time to step back

And wait on the Lord

To give you direction

Do not hold someone new

In your life accountable

For what someone old did

Loving someone

Is doing for them

What you would

Not do for yourself

Always create

Your own

Magic

Fall in love with the man

That always makes

The effort to put a smile

On your face

You must grow as a person

Before you can grow

Anywhere else

You have added another

Dimension to my life

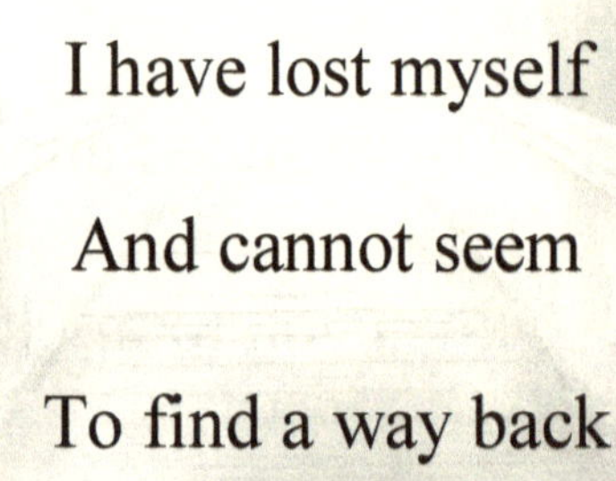

I have lost myself

And cannot seem

To find a way back

The sign to hold on

Is when you put

Your hands together

And pray

Do not use life circumstances

As an excuse

To do what you know

Is wrong

Life is a series of tests

Ever evolving you into the

Person you are meant to be

Every day is a good day

To say a word of praise

Once you understand that everything

You go through has a purpose

It makes coping with life easier

Do not be afraid to ask for help

Your mind, body and heart

Will thank you

Shut out the noise

To listen to

God's still small voice

I live on faith, not religion

Know in your heart

That you always have

Full access to God

Life's happenings

Are teachable moments

From God

To learn life lessons

I love paper

Because it holds the words

I write on it

And displays them

For all the world to see

I will deal with life's punches

As they come

Not one minute before or

One minute after

God may ask a lot of us

But, He has given a lot to us

In moments of trial and tribulation

When darkness takes control

Stay in close proximity

To the Almighty Father

For His hope and grace light the way

The journey is just beginning

Taking one day at time

I am learning to enjoy the ride

Destination unknown

Stay the course

Let God navigate the deep waters

Of your life

No matter how fiercely the wind blows

He brings you safely to shore each time

When you think you have time

And time flies

Make the time

Don't let life pass you by

Let the positivity of your thoughts

Speak words that move you forward

Into action and purpose

THANK YOU FOR READING
"IN MY THOUGHTS"

Write your own quote:

Write your own quote:

Write your own quote:

Write your own quote:

Write your own quote:

For a unique quote, just for you from
the author, send her an email:
virginiamartinauthor@gmail.com

ABOUT THE AUTHOR

Virginia Martin is the Christian author of the Without Borders Inspirational Series. She has attended various writing conferences, author/book events, and regularly goes to writing workshops to perfect her craft. Her passion for writing started at a young age, because she loves to express herself through the written word. Virginia is a member of the Romance Writers of America, and Florida Romance Writers. She has been a Human Resources professional for the past 20 years, and loves helping others. Her future plans are to write her first romance novelette, establish a non-profit community outreach ministry, and continue with her "Share A Word To Make A Difference" initiative. Aside from reading, writing, and basking in the South Florida sun, Virginia enjoys photography, listening to Christian music, and playing Scrabble.
Visit her author blog at:
www.virginiamartinauthor.net

Faith Without Borders: A devotional to inspire you to step out in faith

Volume 1
An inspiring devotional full of scriptural references, thoughts for reflection, and personal testimony that encourages you to step out in faith.

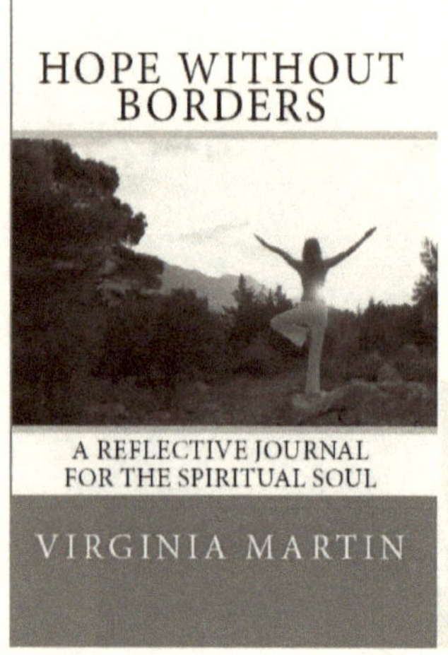

Volume 2
A journal with questions and quotes that
encourage reflective thought, while inspiring your
spiritual soul to record life as it happens.

Love Without Borders: A poetry collection from the heart

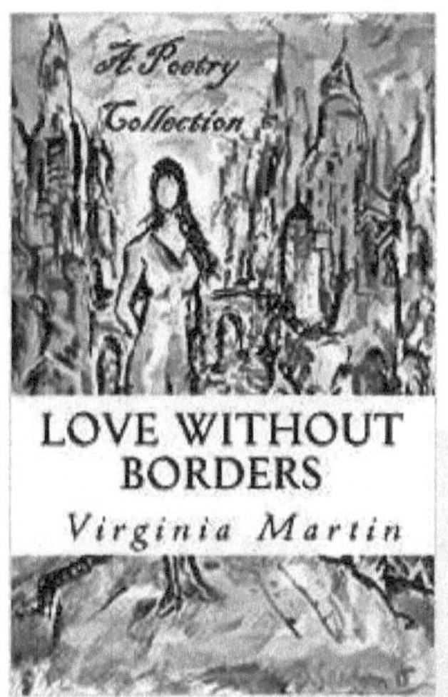

Volume 3
An inspirational poetry collection on faith, hope,
love and life. Open your heart to a new experience
in reading the written word.

Thank you for supporting this book.

If you enjoyed it, please consider sharing it with others by:

- Talking about it on Facebook/Twitter/Instagram

- "LIKE" my Facebook page: www.facebook.com/mywritingself

- Write a book review on Amazon, Goodreads, Barnes and Noble, your website or blog.